Y0-CPC-672

Getting

Dumped

and Getting over It!

DISCARD - WEEDED

By Cylin Busby

PSS!
PRICE STERN SLOAN

To my heartbreak healers:
Jeff B., loan shark of bliss,
Alex R., never afraid,
and to Damon, most of all.—C.B.

ACKNOWLEDGEMENTS
Thank you, thank you, thank you:

I am very grateful to Dr. Elaine Leader at Cedars-Sinai,
who has helped millions of teens through her work at TeenLine
in Los Angeles, and to Dr. Drew Pinsky for his
dedication and expertise.

Special thanks to Jane O'Connor, without whose brilliance
and hard work, there would have been no book and to
Jennifer Frantz, Associate Editor extraordinaire.

Text copyright © 2001 by Cylin Busby. All rights reserved. Published by Price
Stern Sloan, a division of Penguin Putnam Books for Young Readers, New York.
Printed in the United States of America. Published simultaneously in Canada.
No part of this publication may be reproduced, stored in any retrieval system, or
transmitted in any form or by any means, electronic, mechanical, photocopying,
recording, or otherwise without the prior written permission of the publisher.

Library of Congress Cataloging-in-Publication Data is available.

ISBN 0-8431-7679-2 (pbk.)   A B C D E F G H I J
ISBN 0-8431-7712-8 (GB)   A B C D E F G H I J

Plugged In™ is a trademark of Price Stern Sloan.
PSS! is a registered trademark of Penguin Putnam Inc.

Table of Contents

Introduction

It's Over

In this age of instant messaging, cell phones, and fast-paced everything, it's hard to believe there isn't a way to speed up the healing process of a broken heart. But there isn't—we still haven't invented a pill or potion to cure the pain of a bad breakup. It just takes . . . time. This is something that you're going to hear a lot, so get used to it. Everyone—your parents, your best friend, your older sister—is going to say, "It just takes time."

The truth is, having a broken heart sucks. After a few weeks, it starts to suck a little less. But it still hurts. And then it hurts for a while longer. And just when you think you're over him—WHAM! You see him at the school dance, and suddenly you're in the girls' room sobbing

1

to your best friend as if he had just dumped you all over again.

So even though you're going to get tired of hearing that it just takes time, it is the truth. The healing inside your heart will begin. Promise. It's happening right now as you read this, and it will continue to happen. Now turn the page and join some other girls who feel just the way you do . . .

Chapter One

Dumped

It started with an e-mail. He told me he was feeling like maybe we shouldn't go out anymore. I didn't understand. Did he mean that he wanted to slow things down or take a break or what? The next day when I saw him at school, I said, "Can we talk?" and he said sure, and then asked me if I'd gotten the e-mail he wrote me. When I said yes, he said, "Okay, so you know that we're broken up, right?" I was shocked. How could he break up with me over e-mail? After almost a year of going out, he was suddenly acting like someone I didn't even know, and like someone who didn't know me.

—Lucy, 16

When Josh walked into the ice-cream place where I was working, I knew something was up. He looked funny, and he hadn't called me back for two days, which was really weird. I said, "Hi!" and told him how much I missed him. Inside, I had a feeling something bad was about to happen. I was careful not to ask him stuff like "Why haven't you called me?" because I guess deep down, I didn't want to know the answer. He had been acting so different. Finally, he said that since it was summer, he didn't want to be "tied down" with a girlfriend. It was like he had used me and didn't want to be bothered with me anymore. The worst part was, after he broke up with me, he said "Man, I feel so much better now!" Then he walked out.

—Carrie, 17

Whether you see it coming, like Carrie, or are caught by surprise, the way Lucy was, getting dumped is never easy. You've put your trust in someone, fallen in love (maybe even for the very first time) and then, overnight, everything changes. The person you thought you knew is acting totally different, and there's nothing you can do or say to make things go back to the way they were. It's over. You've broken up. He's not your boyfriend anymore. It's so hard. A thousand thoughts race through your head: This can't be happening. I love him. Maybe he'll change his mind. Maybe I can do something to make it better. What did I do wrong? Is there someone else? Why is this happening?

Love Zombie

You don't feel like yourself at all. You get the sensation that the world is spinning, you're going to be sick, like you can't breathe, or you're going to pass out. That's because you're in shock. No matter how it happens, whether he breaks up with you over the phone or by e-mail, you feel shocked for a few minutes as the idea really hits you. You start crying, or you amaze yourself by not crying and hold it in. Even though there aren't any wounds on your body, you're bruised, tender, aching. There is no physical sign of the breakup, but you feel like you've been torn apart. The amount of pain you feel surprises you, and you think that no one else knows just what you're going through. But the physical reaction you're having is totally normal, and it happens to everyone who goes through something traumatic. Look at Maggie's story:

My heart felt like it was literally bleeding. I mean, my chest hurt. I ran into the girls' bathroom and just let it out, I cried harder than I ever have in my whole life. A friend of mine came in to look for me, and I couldn't even tell her what had happened because I was crying so hard. I just remember sitting on the tile floor of the bathroom, and how cold it was. I was thinking: My life is over. My life is totally over.

—Maggie, 15

Why Does it Feel Like This?

Remember how it felt the first time you had a huge crush on a guy? That floating-on-air feeling every time you thought of him, and how you'd almost feel sick with nerves when he walked by? When you talked to him, you'd get so nervous your hands would start sweating and your face would turn red. Some people call that "lovesick." You were so crazy about him, you felt almost ill when you were around him. It's just one way that our emotions can make our bodies actually feel different. It's like going to see a really scary movie: your pulse quickens, you feel your heart beating fast. Then something really frightening happens, and you jump out of your seat—even scream! But nothing has *really* happened to you, you're not in any physical danger, those are just your emotions acting on your body.

The same holds true for when you go through something emotionally traumatic. You cry, you hang your head, maybe you even get mad and feel like breaking something. You *physically* feel the emotions that your head and heart are dealing with. So when you go through something as horrible as a bad breakup with your boyfriend, you definitely feel it in your body. The fun emotion of being in love has been taken away, and in its place is an unbelievable amount of emotional pain. So even though there's no physical evidence or "wound," this pain is very real. As Maggie put it, she felt like she was bleeding, almost as if her boyfriend had literally ripped her heart out.

The key thing to remember is that when you feel this kind of emotional pain, your body has to heal. The pain of heartbreak is like the physical pain of a broken arm, or a deep cut that needs stitches—both need time to heal. And as with a broken arm, the kind of healing your body needs doesn't take place overnight; it takes a while: weeks, or even months.

You'll also be dealing with a whole new set of emotions that come along with a breakup: the embarrassment of having to tell your friends and family, the fear that you're not worthy of love anymore, the pain of having your love rejected by someone you trusted. If your body is dealing with these emotions for the first time, you might not know how to make yourself feel better. You might think, as Maggie did, that you can't go on, that your life must be over. But that's more common than you think. Just listen to what Emma had to say about her first breakup:

When my first real boyfriend broke up with me, I felt like I would never get over him. I cried for months. I could hold it in at school, acting like I had it all together, but inside I was dead. I would wait for my dad to pick me up after school; I'd get in the car and lie on the backseat. I remember thinking, "Now I can finally just cry," and I would. I'd sob the whole way home. My poor dad felt terrible about it, but there was really nothing anyone else could do to make me feel better. Chris was done with me, and I felt like I was done living. Nothing could make me happy.

—Emma, 16

Even though you may not believe it now, the first breakup you go through is the worst. Ask your mom, your dad, your older sister, or cousin about the first time someone broke up with them and they'll tell you the same thing. It's like the first time you do anything: it's scary.

If you've never been on a bike before and suddenly you're put on one and told to ride, you're not going to know what to do and you'll probably get hurt—badly. The next time you're on the bike, you'll try again, remembering what worked the last time, and you'll do better. And the third time you're on the bike, you'll find it even easier. From then on, it only gets better. Love is a lot like that. The first time you fall in love, it's new and wonderful. It's also a little scary. But you're so happy, you don't worry about what might happen. You share yourself entirely with someone else, and he does the same thing back. You are working your way through a romance together. Bliss. But when that love ends, you crash—you're not emotionally prepared to handle it. You have to work through your hurts bit by bit, day by day. And you have to do it alone. You're probably feeling the way Emma did, like nothing matters and nothing will ever make you happy again. But you *will* get over him, and what you're going through now really will make you a stronger person. It won't be easy, and you've got lots of work to do to get better. So let's get started.

Chapter Two

The First
Twenty-Four Hours

The first twenty-four hours after a breakup are
the absolute worst. That's the truth. This is
when you hear things like "You were too good
for him" or "You're better off without him"
over and over again from everyone you know
(and you won't agree with them). You'll
probably also hear the classic remedy for
heartbreak: "It just takes time." This is true,
but actually getting through that time—now
that's the tricky part! You're just starting to deal
with the fact that you're not a couple anymore.
That you're not so-and-so's girlfriend. And
that's the only thing on your mind. Here's a list
of the ten things you need to do right away after
a breakup. You won't get everything on this list

done in the first twenty-four hours, but if you try, you'll be so busy you won't have time to feel sorry for yourself or sit around in your bathrobe all day eating Ben & Jerry's.

Breakup 911: Ten things you need to do right away

1. Get Yourself a Support Friend: Make a list of your top five favorite friends in order, guys or girls, the people you know will be there for you. Then call the first person on your list. If she doesn't know about your breakup, tell her. Then tell her that you're going to need her help for the next few weeks, to be your support friend while you get over this guy. If she says "I'm on the other line, may I call you back?" then consider the #2 person on your list. Go down your list until you find the one friend you know you can count on to be there for you—for middle-of-the-night tearful phone calls and a hug when you need it. Remember, guys get dumped too, so don't forget to put your male friends on your list. If you're embarrassed about calling your friends and asking for help, just put yourself in their shoes: Wouldn't you be honored if your best bud called on you for this kind of support? Sometimes it's okay to be taken care of. If you had the flu, you'd ask your mom to bring you the remote control and a jumbo carton of orange juice without a second thought. This is no different. Be brave enough to ask for help, and big enough to accept it.

2. Steer Clear: Do not go to the pizza joint where you know he hangs out. Do not call his friends and ask them why he broke up with you. And do not go to his soccer game just to cheer him on, the way you always have. You must steer clear of him, his friends, your "special" places, and "your" song for now. Seeing him, especially in the places where you used to hang out together, will make you too sad. You'll be able to handle this kind of thing in the future, but not now, not for the first week or two. This isn't going to be easy to do, but it's important.

3. Let Yourself Be Sad: Even though it's not healthy to sit around all day moping, you do have to take a little time to be just bummed. There's no rule that says you have to jump out of bed with a big smile on your face the day after your boyfriend breaks up with you. You're heartsick, and that's just the same as having the flu: it's worth a day of staying home. If you're tempted to pretend that everything's okay, and that you can handle the pain by hiding it, you're wrong. There's no "burying" the pain of a heartbreak. You either have to deal now or deal later, so get it out. Cry, mope around carrying tissues, and spend some time just feeling sad. And remember that after today, you're a day closer to getting over those blue feelings.

4. Stay Busy: If you don't have a journal or a diary, get one. Start writing about what you're going through, from the beginning. Write down the details of the breakup and how it made you feel. Write a poem or a song. Paint a picture. Write a pretend letter that you will never send to your boyfriend about how he hurt your feelings, and what you're going through. Even though he'll never see the letter, it will make you feel better to get those feelings down on paper.

5. You, You, You: You're feeling bad, and the first person you take it out on is yourself. It's easy to wallow in your sadness. You sit in your room listening to sad songs or you don't even get out of bed. That's okay for the first day after breaking up, but after that, you need to pay special attention to you. Just because you're not so-and-so's girlfriend anymore doesn't mean that you're nobody. You're still a person, and your physical body needs you to take care of it. Even if you're so depressed that you don't want to eat or sleep, remember that your body still needs those things. Try to keep to your regular schedule and find time to work out or exercise. According to Stephanie Gillis, M.A., author of the book *Behind the Body*, working out can actually improve your mood. It's a scientific fact. "When you exercise, your body produces endorphins—those are chemicals released by the brain that make you feel relaxed, happy, and destressed. Working out also helps you sleep better, think clearer, and feel more energized." Sounds good, doesn't it? Try getting a little exercise, even if it's only dancing around in your room to CDs. You'll be surprised at how much a little sweat can lift your spirits.

6. Don't Be Drastic: He always said how much he loved your long hair. Well, you'll show him: you're going to go and have it all chopped off. WAIT! You are not in a healthy state of mind. Any decision you make now is likely to be driven by grief and anger. You're not even thinking about what you want—you're thinking about what you can do to get back at *him*. If you really feel that you need to chop off your hair, or get that nose ring you always wanted, or try a tattoo, wait at least a week or two before you do it. In the time immediately following a breakup, your mind and emotions are out of wack. Your unconscious impulse is to find new things to make you happy or to distract you. But if you do something drastic in this state of mind, you'll only end up making yourself more unhappy. Instead of picturing the look on his face when he sees you with your new short haircut, picture the look on your face when you see yourself in the mirror with your awkward short hair that doesn't actually go with your style (and your ears sticking out). Not pretty. Be patient; the time for making major changes may come. Right now, focus on the real problems.

7. **Memory Lane:** You'll be tempted to go through the old photos or notes he sent you. Don't. You're trying to remember what it was like to be his girlfriend, and to see where things

went wrong. You want to know what happened to the way you used to feel about each other. You won't find the answers in old memories. Put all those notes, poems, photos, mixed tapes, and other stuff away in a box. If you can't trust yourself not to look, give everything to your mom or to your support friend to hide until you feel better. (WARNING: Don't throw out all your old memorabilia of your ex-boyfriend in anger; you'll regret that later. Promise.)

8. Ask for a Hug: Right about now, you need to make contact with the people who care about you. Don't ignore the blinking light on your answering machine because you don't want to talk—call your friends back, make plans with them, get out and be around other people. Even if you know in your head that your friends and family care about you, you should ask for a hug from your mom, your best friend, your cat—the physical contact tells your heart and your body that you are still lovable. The rejection you feel from your boyfriend hurts, and it can make you feel that no one cares about you, or that no one will ever understand you. But that's not true. You're still the same person you were before the breakup. The people who cared about you then care about you even more now. Just let them show it. Get yourself a stuffed teddy bear to sleep with, or buy a new plant to take care of. Show your affection and get loved back. You need it.

9. Mantra: Sounds crazy, but it works. Swear. Make up a reassuring statement about yourself and write it in your journal. It can be something like "I am smart and pretty" or "I'm an amazing girl" or even "I'm worthy of respect and love." If you're having a hard time coming up with something good to say about yourself, think of compliments you've gotten in the past. Has your best friend ever said, "You have a perfect smile"? Or has your teacher told you, "You're a good listener"? That might be your statement right there. At first, you'll probably be embarrassed to write it down, but do it. "After Mark broke up with me," says Joan, "my best friend told me 'You're a hot tamale. You won't be single for long.' I wrote that down in my journal and said it to myself sometimes when I was feeling bummed. It started as a joke, but pretty soon, I started to believe it. Now there's no doubt: I am a hot tamale!" Take it from Joan: When you're feeling down, or when you start thinking about him, say your mantra (out loud or just in your head). Say it enough and you will believe it and become it. *I am a hot tamale . . . I am a hot tamale . . .*

10. Daily Treat: You know that allowance you've been saving for a massive shopping spree? Well, now's the time to break open the piggy bank. When you've gotten through the first twenty-four hours after your bad breakup, it's time to treat yourself. Spend an hour or two at the mini–golf course, buy a new funky face mask and try it with your support friend, maybe even do those special things that you would usually reserve for a birthday celebration—like make a batch of double-chocolate chip cookies just because. You need the cheering up now, so do the things you love best. And keep rewarding yourself in small ways for every day, week, and month you get through after the breakup. You deserve it.

Chapter Three

He Says / She Says

If you could ask your ex anything, what would it be? Probably the big "why?": *Why did you break up with me? Why did you stop caring about me? Why did you leave me for someone else?*

Even if your boyfriend has a solid reason for breaking up with you, it might be hard for him to tell you right now. Also, it might be hard for you to understand. So even though you want to keep asking him "why?" over and over again, or insist that he owes you an explanation, instead, ask yourself something: Is there anything he could say that would make you feel any better, a reason you'd agree with? Probably not, because no matter what the reason, you've still broken up and there's nothing you can do about that. Knowing why isn't going to change the way you feel or miraculously change his mind. Basically, you're not going to like any answer he can give you. As soon as you realize that, you'll stop asking why and start moving on.

But since you're still going to be dying to ask him, we did the work for you. Here, some *other* guys explain what motivated them to break up with girls they were dating. Maybe these stories will help you understand how your ex is feeling, and why he did what he did.

There was this girl, Penny, who sat next to me in study hall. Just to pass the time, we'd send each other these goofy notes with jokes and drawings. Penny really cracked me up. Pretty soon, I was looking forward to study hall every day just to hang out with her. I guess I started liking her without even knowing it. One night I was out with my girlfriend and I just realized that I'd rather be hanging out with Penny all the time, not just in study hall. I knew I had to break up with my girlfriend, but it was so hard. I mean, how do you say:

I like someone else now. Basically, that's what I told her. She still hates me for it.

—Joey, 16

I'm in a band, and my girlfriend used to come and watch us practice. After a couple of weeks, she got bored with listening to us, I guess, and she started making fun of the band. She'd say stuff like "You need to practice guitar more," or "The lead singer is awful." That bugged me because I was really into our practices, I wanted this band to work. Finally, I decided I'd rather have no girlfriend than be with someone who totally didn't get this side of me. So I dumped her, and I never looked back.

—Kenny, 18

I was totally in love with my girlfriend, ever since eighth grade. But all my friends were dating girls who would have sex with them, or at least fool around. And my girlfriend would hardly let me kiss her. When we were in tenth grade, I got tired of it. So I fooled around with this one girl at a party, and then I started going out with her. I still really wanted to be with my girlfriend—she was prettier and cooler than the new girl, but I couldn't take it anymore. So I broke up with her. I think now that it was a mistake, especially since my old girlfriend started dating a friend of mine, and he's psyched to go out with her. It still makes me mad.

—Len, 17

When I was sixteen, I went out with one of my first real girlfriends. She was sweet, and she liked me. That was all I needed. But a few weeks into dating her, I got the sinking feeling that she liked me much more than I liked her. The gap grew and grew, she was inching toward the "L" word while I was rapidly getting annoyed by her. One night I had a long talk with one of her best friends, and I ended up kissing her. Bad move. I got caught. I'm sure my ex-girlfriend still has no idea why I did that to her. I just didn't know how to end things any other way.

—Nick, 20

I had been dating my girlfriend for about six months when something strange happened. This good friend of mine started asking me all these questions about her, like how long we'd been together and was I really into her, that kind of stuff. I thought maybe he wanted to date her. But it turns out that he was gay, and he thought I might be too. At first, I was grossed out by whole idea. I mean, I had a girlfriend! But the more I thought about it, the more I realized he might be right. I was attracted to guys, and I didn't want to admit it to myself. I ended things with my girlfriend, but I couldn't bring myself to tell her the real reason why. I just didn't think she'd understand.

—Matt, 22

Allison was two years younger than I, so when I got

into Harvard I knew it was going to be a problem. I told her I still wanted to keep dating her long distance, but in the back of my head, I kinda knew it wouldn't work out. I guess it was wrong of me to give her any false hope. All through the summer before I left for college I kept trying to break up with her, but we were still having fun so I didn't. Once I moved in at school, I started meeting all kinds of new people, and my life was totally different. Allison was still in high school—going to cheerleader practice and hanging out at the mall. She couldn't relate to my new life. She just kept calling me and e-mailing me these cute little notes. After a while, it made me feel dumb to be dating someone so young. Finally, over Thanksgiving break, I had to tell her it just wasn't going to work out. She kept saying, "You promised me this wouldn't happen!" over and over again. I felt terrible, but once I got back to school, I felt as if a huge weight had been lifted. I could hang out with girls at school and not feel totally guilty about Allison all the time.

—Derek, 21

What's Up with Him?

You felt that you knew him so well, but now that you've broken up, your boyfriend is acting like someone else. What happened to the guy you used to go out with? Remember that guys and girls handle emotional stuff very differently. Some guys have even been conditioned to act a certain way by their guy friends and their fathers—a way that seems totally foreign to girls. According to Dr. Drew of drdrew.com and MTV's *Loveline*, "One predominant difference between men and women is how they deal with relationship termination." While we're more prone to burst into tears, he might go out with his friends and play football to get his feelings out. "This isn't anything personal; it's just biology operating. Women usually prefer to maintain some form of connection with their ex-boyfriends. For men, when it's over, it's OVER. They want women vanished, out of their lives, gone," explains Dr. Drew. So why is your ex acting like that? On the following pages are some strange signs you might see in your former boyfriend, and what they really mean.

You see him: He ignores you or avoids you big-time.

It happens when: He walks by you in the hallway acting as if he has no idea who you are—even though you dated him for eight months!

What it really means: He's acting withdrawn to protect himself from getting hurt. It probably kills him to see you, and it's easier for him to pretend you're not there than to have to deal with you.

You see him: He's angry, or lashing out.

It happens when: He's argumentative with you or his other friends, or you hear that he's been moody and grumpy.

What it really means: If he's getting angry about other things (like slamming his locker door when he's not having a good day), he's just trying to blow off steam. He's not happy, and he doesn't know how else to show it. If he's getting angry or violent with a person (or threatening), that's not okay. He's having a hard time, but he needs professional help to deal with his anger, and you need to tell someone (a teacher or counselor at school, or your parents).

You see him: He blames you for the breakup.

It happens when: You hear through friends that he's saying it was "mutual" or that you broke up with him. Huh?

What it really means: Even though he broke up with you, he can't deal with the problem he's created or take responsibility for it. It's easier for him to say it's your fault—either something you did, or that you wanted to break up. He might even believe it himself. This gives him some distance from the hurt, and he can tell himself he's not responsible, even though he is.

You see him: He acts as though nothing had happened.

It happens when: He comes up to you at school and says "Hi!" as though nothing had ever happened between you. At lunchtime, he sits down next to you and starts munching on a double cheeseburger while you can barely eat, you're still so bummed about the breakup. What gives?

What it really means: Even if he goes about his business as if you had never been a part of his life, or as if the two of you had never been an item, he DOES remember you. Only soap opera characters get that kind of amnesia! Try not to be hurt by his apparent lack of concern. He's probably worried about your feelings, but he can't bring himself to ask how you're doing— he's scared to go there. So he just acts super-friendly instead. He is hurting, too, in some way, even if he can't show it in public. So, when you see him joking with his friends in study hall, or whistling as if he doesn't have a care in the world, know that it's a facade. Think about how hard it must be to have to hide your emotions all the time, and feel sorry for him.

Boys Don't Cry

As Dr. Drew points out, boys and girls are very

different when it comes to handling emotional pain. But that doesn't mean they have no feelings! Even if your ex is acting as if he doesn't have a care in the world, he's got his own set of hurts. Maybe he was dumped once, too, and knows just how it feels. If the male mind is still a mystery to you, these stories from broken-hearted guys will help you see how the other half deals with being dumped.

Amy broke up with me during February, right before Valentine's Day. I went over to my best friend's house to tell him what had happened, and he invited me to go skiing that weekend with his family—to help get my mind off it. I went, but I couldn't stop thinking about the stuff Amy had said to me. I talked my friend's ear off on the trip up to the ski house, and then, while we were there, I know he got sick of hearing me talk about her. It was great to get out on the slopes, but the whole time, I was thinking about her and wondering if there would be a voice mail from her when we got back. Every afternoon when we came down off the mountain, I would be so psyched to check my voice mail, just hoping she had called to change her mind. But then I'd get so bummed when there wasn't a message. It took me a long time to get over her.

—Damon, 17

When Kim decided we shouldn't go out anymore, I tried to convince her that she was wrong. But she had made up her mind; she just kept saying, "Look, it's over." It might sound babyish, but the first person I told was my mom. I guess I was looking for some sympathy. But instead, my mom was bummed, because she really liked Kim. She asked me, "What did you do?" as if it were all my fault! I didn't do anything; I guess Kim just got tired of me. I explained that to my mom, but she just shook her head and looked at me as if I had messed up. I think she still believes I did "something" to make Kim break up with me, which isn't true at all.

—Ken, 16

I had been dating Jess for about a year when we decided we were ready to have sex. I knew that she had tried to do it with her old boyfriend, and that it hadn't been good for some reason. I was a virgin, and we put a lot of planning into the whole thing. I thought it was nice, but after we had sex, Jess changed. She was so worried that I was going to start treating her the way her ex had—and spreading rumors about her at school the way he did—that she dumped me! She wrote me a letter explaining how she felt, and how she couldn't go through that again, but I was still bummed. It was like she wasn't even giving me a chance to be a good guy.

—**Aaron, 18**

Talking to Him

It's going to happen. You go to the same school, you live in a small town, you have mutual friends. You ARE going to see each other again. And when you do, you're going to have no idea what to say. If there's still unfinished business between you, there might be some uncomfortable post-breakup conversations that you'll have to get through. Here are some true stories from girls who have been there, and what they recommend to help you deal (bravely) with an ex.

When I saw Eric for the first time after we broke up, it just killed me. I just stood there and cried, right in the middle of the hallway. I didn't care anymore. He was trying to talk to me, but I couldn't listen. Then he said, "Look, I never meant to hurt you like this." I said the first thing that came into my head: "Well, you did hurt me. And you still have to deal with it." That shut him up.

—**Lucy, 16**

I told Mark that I couldn't believe that someone who loved me would treat me this way. That's when he said, "I never told you I loved you." I was shocked. I

said, "I loved you, and I thought you felt the same way.
I guess I was wrong about you." That seemed to hurt
him, especially since I was willing to confess how I felt.

                                                —Maggie, 15

I knew that Joe and Cathy had already started
going out. So when I saw him again, I just said,
"How could you do this to me? How could you
dump me for her?" His only answer was "I like her.
What am I supposed to do about it?" He was acting
like it wasn't his fault, like falling for her was something he had no control over. All I could think about
was how selfish he was being—like a baby who just had
to have something right away. So I told him that, and
he surprised me by saying he was sorry—and that I was
right!

                                                —Kim, 17

Tommy had this group of friends that I had never
liked—they were a bunch of druggies from what I could

tell, and they got on my nerves. Tommy knew that I didn't like them, so we rarely hung out with them. But when he broke up with me, that was one of his excuses—that I didn't like his friends. I was shocked! It wasn't like I had ever tried to hide the fact that I didn't get along with this group of people. I told him, "I'm not dating your friends. This is between you and me. Don't blame them for your problems." He didn't seem to get it, but it made me feel better to say it.

—Beth, 16

After we broke up, Kev admitted that he had cheated on me with this senior girl a few months back. It was like he had to tell me everything at the end, maybe so that I wouldn't like him anymore. I just said, "Thanks for letting me know that I can never trust you, and that I didn't really know you at all." He was shocked. I think he had expected me to cry and beg him to come back. But that's really how I felt.

—Suzanne, 18

Chapter Four

Facing the World

I only told my mom and my best friend when Chris dumped me. I just kept thinking that he would change his mind, so why should I tell the world what we were going through? Then this sophomore girl who had a crush on him came up to me in the hall and asked me if it was true that Chris and I had broken up. I was shocked. If she knew about it, there was only one person who could have told her: Chris. And all I could think about was why he had told her. I guess he wanted to go out with her. That was when I realized it must really be true. It was like hearing about it for the first time all over again.

—Emma, 16

Spreading the Word

Dealing with your breakup is one thing; telling other people about it is another. It's not going to be easy to tell people about what happened to you. You probably won't be able to tell your mom or your best friend without crying, and that's okay. You're still dealing with the initial shock and the pain, and you're letting it out as you talk about your feelings. That's good; you should cry.

But sooner or later, you'll have to go back to school. Even if it's summertime, you're going to bump into people you know. Other friends of yours—or his—might not have heard yet that you and your boyfriend have broken up. You're going to have to tell them. Even if they already know, you may be asked other hard questions. Here's a list of the some of the questions you might encounter, and how to handle them.

"Is it true that you and Mike broke up?"
How you answer this question depends on who's

asking it. If, like Emma, you're being asked by a girl who you know is interested in your ex-boyfriend, it's going to be tough to keep your cool. If you're being asked by a good friend, then it's an opportunity to ask for support.

If it's his friend asking you the question, say: "It's true, but I'm surprised he didn't tell you himself. I guess he's not feeling so good about it either."

If it's a girl who's after your ex, say: "It's true that we're going through some stuff right now, but I really don't want to talk about it with you." It's okay to be a little rude here because she's being way rude by asking you, and she probably knows it. Just don't lash out, or threaten her in any way. Remember, it's not her fault that you guys broke up, but she could show a little sympathy.

If it's a friend or an adult whom you can trust: "Yeah, and I'm really bummed about it. So if you see me acting weirdly, that's probably why." This is an opportunity for you to ask for help, if you need it, so don't hesitate to say: "Do you have any advice for how to get over him?" Or: "I'd like to talk to you about it, if you have time."

"What's Up?" or "What's Wrong?"

When you run into people who have no idea about the breakup, it's in your best interest to tell them. They might be able to offer you some support, and saying it out loud actually helps you deal with the reality of it a little bit better. If you're thinking of keeping your breakup a secret, think again: your friends and acquaintances will be able to tell that something's wrong (unless you are a truly fabulous actress), and they'll be wondering what's going on with you. Friends who care about you might even be offended if you're secretive and they find out the truth later through someone else. Honesty is the best policy, even if it's not easy.

For the first few days after your breakup,

don't be surprised if you burst into tears or feel like crying when you tell people about it. Just saying those few words can bring on a flood of emotions (just the way the three little words *I love you* bring on so many feelings). To avoid a public meltdown, you might want to practice saying this phrase a few times to yourself: "We broke up" or "Mike and I broke up." This will prepare you to say it to others and will also help you accept the reality. Other things you can say: *"I'm sorry if I seem kinda out of it. Mike and I broke up, and I'm feeling really bummed." "My boyfriend and I broke up, and I'm really down." "Sorry if I don't seem like myself, but my boyfriend and I just broke up and it's taking me a while to get over it."*

"Why did you guys break up?" or "What happened? You were the perfect couple!"

These kinds of questions are the toughest because you don't have an answer for them. Actually, you might be asking these questions yourself, so it makes it really hard also to hear them from someone else. You do need to come up with an answer, because people are going to ask you what happened and you don't want to completely lose it when they do.

If you're wondering yourself why he broke up with you, don't say: *"I don't know. Why don't you ask Mike. He's the one who dumped me!"*

This will just make you feel worse, and it will scare your friends instead of making them feel that they can help you.

Instead say: *"I wish I knew. I guess it just wasn't working out. I'm still really hurt."* At this point, you aren't a couple anymore, so you can't speak for him (and you shouldn't speak against him). All you can do is tell people how *you* feel.

If you do know why he broke up with you, don't say: *"Mike wanted to go out with some slut in his study hall, so he dumped me to get with her."*

If you know he dumped you for someone else, or just to be single for a while, you are not obligated to tell anyone else that. It's your business, not theirs. You can say: *"We weren't right for each other anymore"* or *"We just couldn't work things out"* or even *"We wanted different things."*

These are all true, and it saves you from looking like a bitter, unwanted ex-girlfriend with an axe to grind.

"Do you think you might get back together?"

Ouch. Some people can be so unkind, without even knowing it. If you're asked this question, the best answer is *"I don't know."* Or *"I don't think so."* Simple. Don't say: *"If we don't, I'm going to kill myself"* or *"Once he comes to his senses, I'm sure we will."*

These are totally unhealthy thoughts, and you shouldn't even let your mind go there. It's normal at this point to fantasize that you two might get back together, but you shouldn't say it out loud—that will just solidify it in your head and make you dream about something that probably won't happen. Plus, if you keep day-dreaming that you might get back together, you're not really working on getting over him. We'll deal more with this in chapter 7.

"Would you mind if I went out with Mike now?"

If you live in a small town or have a small group of friends, someone might actually ask you this. A friend or an acquaintance of yours might want to date your ex. Or she might actually be asked out by your ex and come to you first to make sure it's okay. This is a very tough situation, especially if it happens soon after your breakup. What can you say? Of course you mind! But you can't say "If you go anywhere near Mike, I'll put an evil curse on you both." So how do you handle this situation? You could try being honest: *It would hurt me to see Mike with anyone right now. But I can't tell you what to do.* Or, if you're really hurt by what he's doing, it's okay to say the obvious: *What Mike does is really none of my business anymore.*

If this girl is a friend of yours, it's time to consider how much her friendship means to you. Consider this: Would you do the same thing to her? Probably not, because you know now how much a heartbreak hurts. Maybe she doesn't understand how you feel. You can tell her that you are counting on her, as a friend, to be supportive: *"Mike broke my heart, and I could use your support. If you're dating him, I don't think I could go to you for help."* Or even: *"Mike really hurt me, and I hope you understand that. Maybe you're too busy thinking about what you want to see how bad I feel right now."*

It might be hard for you to keep your cool if a friend does ask you this question. That's a normal reaction. If you need time to think about it before you answer, say so: *"I can't believe you're asking me that. I need time to think about it."* Or: *"I'm still feeling really fragile from our breakup, so I don't think I can give you an honest answer."*

Whatever question you're faced with, in whatever situation, the only way to prepare yourself is to practice. If you have to, look in a mirror and ask yourself each of the above questions. Then think of a good answer that you're comfortable with and practice saying it out loud. Even if you're never asked for real, you'll be helping yourself by getting some of those feelings out in the open.

Hello, Visine

It's never easy to face the world after something bad—like a breakup—has happened. Getting yourself mentally prepared, like practicing what you're going to say, can help. There are also some tricks to help you look as if you've got it all together, even though inside you're still feeling down. And if you look better, you will feel better. Guaranteed.

Before you head back to school or work or out into the world after your breakup, you should put together a little "breakup emergency kit" that you can carry in your backpack or your purse. This kit can go with you anywhere, and help you face obstacles that you might encounter while you're still getting over him. Find a makeup bag, or go out and buy yourself a new one as a treat, and put some of these items into it:

1. Tissues: One of the small travel-size packs will fit, and you'll find them handy if you have a tearful moment (or if you suddenly develop an allergic reaction to your ex and have a huge sneezing fit!).

2. Eyedrops: If you spend study hall in the bathroom crying, no one needs to know but you. Drop some Visine in your eyes, and you'll look better instantly. If you wear contacts, remember to remove them before using the Visine. Once the drops are in, you can return your contacts.

3. Makeup: Carry an extra tube of your concealer (to cover up under-eye circles) and a tube of waterproof mascara. (Waterproof is the key—it's sob-proof and tear-resistant!) Also be sure to have a lip gloss or lipstick that you really like on hand. A fresh coat of lipstick or colored gloss can make you feel like a new woman, ya know?

4. Note from your support friend: If your friend has written you a nice note or sent you a great e-mail, print that out and carry it with you too. You'd be surprised how good it can make you feel to read something like that when you're feeling down, even if it's just a funny "I'm so bored in study hall" note.

5. Pack of gum: Get the big value pack of your favorite kind of gum. One piece will give you a mini-lift and take your mind off your troubles for a minute. When you can't run to the bathroom for a good cry, try a piece of gum. No joke, it works.

6. Photo: Carry a picture of your dog, your mom, your teddy bear, you and your best friend . . . or whatever will make you smile and know you are loved ('Cause you are!).

7. Bonus item: If you have an item that symbolizes your worth—the spelling bee medal you won, an exam or report card you're proud of, anything that says you are bigger and better than this one glitch in your love life—then add that to your kit as well.

Tuck the whole thing into your backpack or purse and remember it's there if you need it. If you feel as if you're about to burst into tears, or if you're so sad you just want to go home and watch soaps all day, take a deep breath and go somewhere you can be alone for a minute instead. Take out your kit and have a good cry, then read your note and look at your picture. Pick yourself back up, and get back out there. Remember that you have the kit with you if you need it. Just knowing it's there might make you feel better.

The emergency kit also makes a great idea for a friend of yours, if she goes through a bad breakup. You can put one together for her and give it to her as a gift. Just think about how great you would have felt if someone had done that for you. It would mean a lot.

Chapter Five

What Did I Do Wrong?

Is it the way you look, your clothes, the fact that you weren't ready to have sex yet, or that you had sex too soon—why did he dump you? WHY? If you're playing the blame game by trying to figure out what you did wrong, you're wasting your time. It's not you who changed; it's him. He's planted these seeds of self-doubt in your head—even if he didn't do it on purpose.

Think about it this way: Your boyfriend used to tell you that you were beautiful and special, the most amazing girl ever. Even if he didn't give you tons of compliments, he showed you that he thought you were cool just by going out with you. That's a great feeling, to know that someone you're crazy about likes you back and wants to date you. So what happened? Why did things change? Why did he suddenly change his mind about you?

You're probably thinking that it has to be something about you that's changed, that you're not special or beautiful anymore. Wrong! The only thing that changed was his mind. This is one of the hardest things to deal with about a breakup, but you have to let go of the idea that you did something wrong. Even if you did screw up somehow, and he used that as an excuse to dump you, you need to realize that making mistakes is human, everyone does it. Would you break up with him if he made a simple mistake? Not if you cared about him. You'd probably forgive him, or work through the problem and move on. So don't overanalyze every tiny mistake you made while you guys were going out, or criticize your every imperfection. Blaming yourself for the breakup is super-unhealthy, and it will only make you feel worse. Even if you can pinpoint one thing that you did wrong, you need to forgive yourself and move on to get over this guy and get better. Here are some of the most popular ways girls put the blame on themselves—and how to turn that blame game around.

"I didn't do the stuff he wanted to do."
Your boyfriend likes to hunt deer, and you are a card-carrying member of PETA. Obviously, you're going to refuse to go hunting with him, even if he looks supercute in his army fatigues and his big orange cap. If he can't understand that you have your own views about issues in the world, then he's not the right guy for you—that's the simple truth. If you and your ex-boyfriend had a lot of different interests—or even came from two different cliques at school—it's up to both of you to find ways to enjoy each other's hobbies and habits or meet in the middle.

Jeff was a football player, but I'm just not a big fan. After we'd been going out for a few months, I would go to his games sometimes and cheer for him, but even then I didn't really understand what was going on in the game. Then he asked me to start coming to his practices after school—honestly, I had no interest. Besides, I'm on the school paper, so I couldn't make it to another after-school activity. He said it was a sign that I wasn't really into our relationship, which wasn't true at all. He dumped me and started dating one of the cheerleaders two weeks later.

—Natalie, 17

What about the stuff *you* like to do? Did he ever join you shopping at the mall or come to your soccer game? Don't blame yourself for not liking all the same things that he likes—it would be positively inhuman if the two of you agreed on everything. Think about it: Even you and your best best friend don't agree on absolutely everything. Maybe she likes pop music and you won't listen to anything but rap. Does that mean you'd stop hanging out with her? If your boyfriend broke up with you over something as small and silly as that, and he wasn't willing to even try to compromise, maybe you guys were not the ideal couple you thought you were. Either that, or he's a jerk and you're better off without him.

"I wouldn't have sex or go as far as he wanted to."

If your boyfriend is ready for sex, and you aren't, it can be seen as a good test of the relationship. Love is built on mutual respect, so he shouldn't pressure you or threaten to break up with you if you aren't willing to do what he wants to do sexually. If he won't wait, he doesn't really care about you as a person. According to Ned Vizzini, author of the book *Teen Angst? Nahhhh*, "Guys who break up with girls just because they won't have sex are sort of like sexual predators." It's not about you anymore. It's about him getting sex from someone—anyone. And you'll probably see your ex-boyfriend dating someone else, someone who will do what he wants sexually. But don't feel bad about this, or think that you made a mistake by choosing not to have sex. If you're ever in doubt, Ned adds: *"When you see him around in the hallways, remember one thing: If all he's looking for is sex, he's opening himself up to all sorts of sexually transmitted diseases. And by being dumped, you're saving yourself from catching anything from him."*

'Nuff said.

"I was too clingy/demanding."

Sometimes a boyfriend will break up with a girl by telling her that he needs more "space" or that she's too demanding of his time. In a healthy relationship, you have time for each other and time for yourselves. It's not all your fault if he was feeling suffocated, especially if he didn't say anything about it until the end of the relationship.

If you're thinking that you *were* too demanding of him, just cancel those thoughts out by remembering all the things you did right—like giving him the time to hang out with his guy friends or play Nintendo games when you were more in the mood to watch a TV movie. And there were certainly times when he enjoyed the time you spent with him—like the night you skipped the school dance together to go out for a romantic dinner, or when you lavished gifts on him on Valentine's Day.

A lot of guys have a hard time articulating the difference between what's a good amount of attention from a girlfriend and what's too clingy. Short of being a mind reader, there's no way you could have known that you were acting too clingy for him. Also, a lot of guys will use this excuse for a breakup when they can't put their real feelings into words. They're afraid to say how they feel, so instead they blame it on you—and say that you were "too clingy" or demanded too much time and attention. Think it through before you blame yourself for something you're probably not guilty of.

"I pushed him away/I was scared."

Maybe he told you that he loved you, and you weren't ready for that. Or he wanted to see you more often than you wanted to see him. Or the relationship was moving too fast for you. He might have told you, "Well, if you can't handle it, then we're not right for each other." But he's wrong and this just shows how little he knows about you. It's human to be scared in an intimate relationship, and someone who cares about you will know that and slow down. "This is a push-and-pull system," says Dr. Judy, the relationship psychologist behind *MyDrJudy.com*. "When one person pulls away, the other person's instinct is to cling more tightly." So is there a solution to this relationship conflict? You can get out of the push and pull by simply saying to yourself, "I do not want to be in a situation where we don't want the same thing. It's best for me to move on." And remember: Just because you and your boyfriend weren't a perfect match, that doesn't mean this breakup is your fault.

"How could I have been so dumb! I never should have gone out with him."

Why on earth did you ever trust that guy? Now you can see that he was lying to you the whole time and dating other girls, or using you. But you're still hurting because you fell in love—even if you fell in love more with your idea of him than the real him. Your pride is hurt, and you don't know why, but you still want him back—or at least the "him" that you thought you knew.

When I started dating Matthew, friends of mine at school warned me about him. They said that he was a cheater, and that he was only looking to hook up. But he was different with me, we were really in love. Or so I thought . . . As it turned out, my friends were right. When Matt found out that I wouldn't have sex with him, he dropped me and acted like he never knew me. So much for love.

—Josie, 16

It's human to love, and it's normal to trust others. You're not the person who messed up here; he is. Still, it feels as if you're being punished. But remember that your only crime was trusting someone who ended up lying to you or breaking your heart. Don't tell yourself that you won't trust or won't love anyone else. There are plenty of good guys out there, so don't rule them all out just because you happened to fall for one bad egg. Let yourself heal, stop blaming yourself, and you'll meet someone who is worthy of your affection when you're ready. And don't call yourself stupid; you're just learning the ways of love.

If You Went There: Sex

You might have thought that sex was a big deal during your relationship, but it's an even bigger deal after your breakup. If you had sex with your ex-boyfriend, then you were in a very intimate relationship—with far more serious implications. You probably only considered pregnancy or STDs as the dangers of a sexual relationship. But there are emotional attachments and problems that come along with intimacy, too. As you get to know and trust someone, you show him more and more about yourself. You introduce him to your friends, then to your family, then you show him things about yourself—maybe stuff that no one else knows. Being intimate deepens your love and makes you feel more attached to him. But when the relationship is over, it also adds a whole new level of pain to your breakup. The saying goes, "The bigger the love, the bigger the hurt."

I lost my virginity to my boyfriend, and three months later we broke up. I had been through breakups before, but this time it was awful. I kept thinking about how well he knew me—that he had seen me naked, and I had taken a shower with him, and we'd had sex. I couldn't believe that now he was going to go and do all of those things with some other girl. That's

*what really bothered me. It was so special, and now
it seemed like it meant nothing.*

                                     —Carol, 17

Once you've been intimate with someone
the way Carol was, it's even harder to deal with
the end of the relationship. Like Carol, you
might have a very tough time getting over the
fact that this is the person you lost your
virginity to, or whom you've had sex with. It
seems like a bond that's so special, and beyond
just the regular high-school dating stuff—and
that's because it is. Obviously, sex is far more
physically bonding than just holding hands,
and it's much more emotionally bonding, too,
because of the feelings that we, as human
beings, attach to it. It takes a mature person to
be able to handle the emotions that come with
being intimate, especially after a breakup.

If you did have sex with your ex and now
you regret it for whatever reason, you need to
forgive yourself, learn from this painful

experience, and move on. Now you know that sex can make a relationship closer—but that's a blessing and a curse. Though it can feel wonderful to be that close to someone, the bond you create is much harder to break later. It might be a good idea to talk to an older person whom you trust about your feelings—a big sister, older cousin, even a friend at school who's been in an equally serious relationship. They can give you advice, plus it may make you feel better to know that you're not the only one who has been through this deep emotional hurt. In the future, remember that you can't allow yourself to be that emotionally and physically exposed to anyone unless you are really ready for *all* the consequences.

If you didn't have sex with your ex, but are still considering it with future boyfriends, bear in mind what this chapter has covered, and reread Carol's quote above. As hard as your breakup was, it could have been harder. Remember that, and save sex for a time when you are emotionally ready for the responsibility.

Chapter Six

Getting Even

After you've had a good cry over your breakup and have grown tired of blaming yourself for his mistakes, the anger usually sets in. You want revenge, you want to lash out... and five minutes later you want to hug your teddy and just cry again. You're alternating between being spitting mad and a tearful crybaby. What's up with that? "When someone we have trusted hurts us, it's very common to experience mixed emotions toward that person," says Dr. Elaine Leader, a psychotherapist and the founder of *TeenLine* in Los Angeles, California. "The sense of betrayal evokes anger, and the loss of trust makes us feel sad. But whether you're feeling sad or mad, the process you're going through still hurts."

The most important thing to do now is to get in touch with your feelings, rather than trying to hide them. According to Dr. Leader, "If we allow ourselves to go through these difficult times without running away from the intensity of the feelings, we ultimately emerge a stronger and wiser person." But dealing with your overwhelming anger isn't always easy or safe. Here are some guidelines to follow that will help you work through your moments of sheer fury and get revenge the right way.

The Wrong Kind of Revenge

You lash out at your ex. Maybe you say mean things, or call his house and hang up. You might be tempted to do more. It's totally normal to fantasize about giving his car a few flat tires, or getting your older brother to beat him up. It's when you actually *act* on those fantasies that you get yourself into trouble. Even though you're so mad you can't stand it, you've got to channel your anger into less harmful means. There are a few key reasons why it's a good idea to keep your anger and desire for revenge under control.

You'll look bitter and pathetic: If you put a big sign on his locker announcing to the school that he's a jerk for breaking up with you, you're only going to make yourself look bad. Don't give people any more reason than they already have to ask questions about your breakup, or to feel sorry for you. If you carry a grudge too long, you'll appear desperate and slightly insane. Remember, you are not defined by this person—you are your own woman. Don't make yourself the subject of ridicule at school. Keep your evil feelings about your ex to yourself, or share them only with your close friends.

I was so mad at Casey when we broke up that I did something really stupid. I called every pizza place in town and ordered delivery to his house—I must have sent seven or eight large pizzas over there! I was picturing his face as he opened the door to find the pizza delivery guy, and then to have it happen again and again. Hilarious, right? Except for the fact that

Casey wasn't home that night. His parents were so mad when they found out who was responsible, and then everyone at school found out. I looked like a jealous, immature baby.

—Heather, 18

You'll be sorry later: When you first break up with a guy, you're not yourself. You're a love zombie, and you're not emotionally ready to handle a lot of things. Revenge is one of them. So, just like that radical haircut you're dying to get, you have to wait until you're emotionally calmer. Then reconsider your impulses. If you're thinking of calling his mom and telling her how her son cheated on the history exam, or you're tempted to have your big brother "discuss" the breakup with your ex-boyfriend, don't. Please give yourself more time before you act. In a matter of days or weeks, you'll think better of the idea and wonder how you could have ever felt that way. If you're still feeling that you want your big brother to beat him up a month after your breakup, it's time to see a therapist and get through your anger in a professional way.

You'll go to jail: That's right. A lot of the revenge tactics floating around in your head are illegal. These include, but are not limited to: scratching his car or flattening his tires, crank-calling his house, stealing and damaging any of his property, telling lies about him to authorities (like the police or teachers at school), threatening him or anyone in his family . . . the list goes on. Do you really want to earn a police record because some jerk broke up with you? He's done enough harm already. Use your head. If you're really feeling as if you're about to lash out and do something terrible, check out the following list called "The Right Kind of Revenge." If that still doesn't work, call your support friend, or tell your parents. They can help you work through your anger in a more constructive way.

The Right Kind of Revenge

You know how you've always heard that girls mature faster than boys? Well, it's true. You're way ahead of him. That's one reason why you don't have to resort to petty crimes and annoying behavior to get even with your ex. In fact, you don't have to involve him at all! This secret method will leave you looking and feeling better than crank-calling his house. It's called "Getting Even the Smart Way," and here are the four steps to making it work:

Concentrate on you: Maybe you've heard the old expression "The best revenge is success." If it doesn't make a lot of sense, think of it this way: The best revenge you can get against your ex is to look great and move on. He won't believe it when he sees you at the mall, looking great and with another guy. He'll start thinking, "Why did I ever break up with her?" So take your angry energy that you could direct at him and use it to work on yourself.

When Josh dumped me, I was devastated. I worked in an ice-cream store, and I think I covered my sadness with eating. I had a couple of hot fudge sundaes every day. (I'm not kidding!) I gained about ten pounds and all the dairy made my face break out, so that just made me feel worse about myself. I woke up one day and couldn't fit in my jeans. I felt so sick of myself, I knew I had to do something. So I talked to my mom, and she suggested that I start running with her in the mornings. It wasn't easy— my mom can run five miles, and I could barely make it through fifteen minutes at first! But I stayed with it. By the end of the summer, I was in better shape than when Josh had been dating me. And I guess by focusing on myself, and talking to my mom, I had been able to move past what he had done to me. I went back to school a new girl.

—Carrie, 17

Karma Rule: Karma is the belief that for every

action there is an equal and opposite reaction. According to Dr. Jonn Mumford, author of the book, *Karma Manual: 9 Days to Change Your Life*, "A precise definition of Karma emphasizes that every activity, be it mental or emotional or simply a physical action in the world, has a consequence. Karma is, if you wish, an equivalent of physics—as far as you push the pendulum in one direction, it is going to swing back in an equal arc on the other side."

So, in the world of breakups, relationship Karma means that if he broke your heart, someone will break his heart in the future. Then he'll know the pain he put you through, and perhaps he'll be sorry. You may not be there at the time—you might not even know him anymore. But it will happen, and eventually he will have to pay for the emotional pain he dealt you. The key to Karma is keeping things on the up-and-up. Don't wish or hope that something bad happens to him. Just know that it will happen, and move on from there.

Photo Doctor: So you've got this whole photo album filled with photos of the two of you in happier days—at homecoming in your new dress, on the school field trip, goofing around at the beach. Believe it or not, when you do get over your old boyfriend for good, you'll probably want these pictures. They'll remind you of your first serious love, or a great time in your life, or just someone you were once very close to. So just as you wouldn't throw out pictures of your best friend after she moved away, you shouldn't throw these pictures of you and your ex out, or damage them.

If your anger overcomes you and you just can't stand to look at his sneaky smirk anymore, take a few of the pictures of you two together and perform a minor operation on them. Using a pair of scissors, carefully cut him out of the picture, leaving yourself and anyone else in the photo untouched. As you throw his half of the picture in the trash, tell yourself that you are tossing out all your hurt and pain. Say it out loud: "I'm throwing away all the pain you caused me." This may sound silly, but it really works. Again, don't cut up all your pictures; save some in a place where you don't have to see them or be reminded of them (or give your photo album to your mom or your best bud to hold for you until you're feeling better). The symbolic act of "tossing" him into the trash will probably make you feel a little bit better about your old boyfriend and help you rid yourself of the hurt.

The X Game

This game is for two players, you and your best friend. So invite over your best bud and get ready to play.

Here's what you'll need:

    two pieces of white paper

    one large black marker

    one roll of toilet paper

    water

    tape

First, think about anything that used to bother you about your ex-boyfriend. Maybe he chews with his mouth open, or he bites his nails. Maybe he had more serious faults: for example, he lied to you, or tried to pressure you to have sex. Whatever you didn't like about him, write it all down in a list on one piece of paper, and number the list. When you get done, put that list off to the side and get the second piece of paper. Now draw a picture of his face, emphasizing your least favorite thing about him. If you couldn't stand that his bangs were always too long, draw them even longer—like down to his chin. If his braces got on your nerves, make sure they take up half his face, and add a little spinach between his two front teeth. When you're done with your drawing, put it up on the wall, with the face side looking at you. Tape it in place.

Remember the numbered list? How many items did you list? Rip off one small sheet of t.p. for each item on your list. Roll the sheet into a ball and use a little water on it (you've just made a spitball). If you haven't had any previous experience with spitballs, they stick well to almost anything. Toss one at the picture of your ex-boyfriend, and you'll see—or shoot it through a straw for more accuracy. If you want, you can say out loud what each spitball is for, reading from your list as go.

After you and your best friend get done throwing stuff at your ex, you'll both feel a lot better. Take down his picture and throw it and the list away right after you're done. Tell yourself as you throw the papers out that you're tossing out all the pain he caused you, and that you're moving on. Works like magic.

The New Girlfriend

Not only did you get dumped, but you were dumped for someone else. That adds a whole new level of hurt to the situation. Instead of having just one person to be mad at, you have two. And if he dumped you for someone else, you're probably feeling more angry at her than

you are at him for what happened. But before
you switch her shampoo with a big bottle of
Nair, stop and think about it.

Don't confront her: You can't wait to tell his
new girlfriend EXACTLY what you think of
her. But remember, she's not the problem, he
is. Remind yourself of the facts: you were in a
relationship with him, not her. He's the person
you put your trust in, the person you believed
in. You might not even have known this girl
before he started going out with her, and she
probably didn't know anything about you. So
why are you blaming her for what happened?
Because it's easier to take it out on someone
anonymous than on the person you were in love
with, your old boyfriend. You might even try to
convince yourself that she "stole" him from you,
or tricked him into leaving you. Not true, and
deep down you know it. A person's affections
can't be stolen. The fact is, he fell for another
girl, and that just shows that his love for you

couldn't be trusted—even more reason to be rid of him.

Don't stalk her or them: You just want to see if he's taking her to the same movie theater that you guys used to go to. Or you want to find out if his new girlfriend has gone over to his house after school. So you cruise by his place to see if her car is parked in the driveway. Innocent, right? Nope, it's creepy and wrong. Put yourself in this situation: What if you started dating this great new guy. On your second date at the movie theater, some weird girl walks up to you and starts yelling at both of you, going on and on about how the guy you're with dumped her, and what a witch you are. Your date is looking mortified. Now how does it feel? Everybody has ex-girlfriends and ex-boyfriends out there—let them stay in the past. And if you're the ex-girlfriend, don't try to ruin your boyfriend's new relationship. It won't work—actually, it will probably just bring them closer together, and you'll end up looking like an idiot. So steer clear of him and her, at school or anywhere else, until you feel that you can see him with someone else and not lose it.

I heard that my ex, José, was dating someone else right after we broke up. I got really suspicious and I was dying to know if it was true. So I waited around after school one day and then broke into his locker (I knew his combination). I went through everything—all his papers, books, notebooks—looking for a clue. Just then, a teacher came down the hall. I tried to play it off like I was just looking for something in a friend's locker, but I was busted. I ended up getting detention for a week, plus they told José about it. He and his new girlfriend treated me like I was a crazy stalker for the rest of the year.

—**Raina, 17**

Don't compare yourself with her: She

makes all A's and you've never been on the honor roll. Or you're the one with the good grades, and she's the one who stayed back in sixth grade. So what? Don't compare your good or bad traits with your ex's new girlfriend's. Think about the best-case scenario: you're prettier than she is, you're smarter than she is, and you're better than she is. But guess what? He's still with her, and not you. So whether you win or lose the comparison game, you're still going to feel awful. Either he left you for someone you think is "better" than you (which hurts), or he left you for some loser and you have no idea why he's dating her (which also hurts). So instead of focusing on her and what she's got that you don't, work on yourself as we recommended earlier in this chapter. That's a much faster and more productive way to start moving on.

Chapter Seven

Getting over Him

The shock is gone. You can face the facts now: He dumped you. It's really over. So why are you still thinking about him and crying every day? Believe it or not, you're about halfway to the point of being totally over him. The tough part now is to keep moving in the right direction. Here are some tips for dealing with the tough times, and getting through them without moving backward on your breakup recovery.

Speed Dial Danger

Your hand is on the phone. Or you're ready to press the *send* button on that e-mail. You've just got to reach out and tell him how you feel. Here are the top three reasons why you're dying to get in touch with him, and how to hold back.

What to do when you want to tell him off: How could he? How dare he! And now he's dating HER? What about all the stuff you heard that he's been saying about you behind your back? You have to confront him and tell him what a jerk he is—tell him that you hate his guts and hope you never have to see him ever again. Right? Wrong. Your emotions are in turmoil right now, and you're really not yourself. Just like plotting to get your revenge, calling him to yell at him is a really bad idea. If you call him now and say something mean, you will regret it later. Plus, stirring up all that anger will only set you back on your course of getting over him. Just look at Sara's story of speed-dial danger:

One Sunday afternoon, I just couldn't take it anymore. I was sitting on my bed, writing in my journal about Perry and how he had dumped me, and I got so mad. I looked over at the phone and just jumped off the bed and dialed his number before I could stop myself. His brother answered, and I guess he recognized my voice. He put down the phone and I heard him call Perry and say, "It's Sara." Then he came back on and said Perry "isn't home." Sure. When I hung up, I was so mad my hand was shaking. After everything we'd been through, he wouldn't even take my call. I wish I hadn't called him so I didn't have to know that, it hurt so bad.

—Sara, 16

If you're really really mad at him and you think you've just got to tell him, then do it—but do it in a letter. Write down everything you want to say to him, everything you want him to know. Now here's the catch: *Don't mail it.* Fold it up and stick it in your journal or your sock drawer. Just as we told you in the second chapter, you'll feel better just for having gotten those emotions out. And now you can move on.

What to do when you really really really have to ask him why he broke up with you . . . again:

You read chapter 3, and you know you shouldn't ask him why, but now that you've accepted the breakup and you're not "mad" anymore, you just really need to have a reason. Why did he break up with you? Your first step is to go back and read chapter 3 again. Look over some of those reasons that guys gave for breaking up with a girlfriend. They range from the serious (he broke up with her for another girl) to the lame (he just wanted more time to hang out with the guys). But whatever reason he gives you, it's just not going to be good enough. Focusing on the "why" of the breakup at this stage isn't going to do you any good. The bottom line is he broke up with you because he didn't want to be with you anymore, that's why. Now you have the answer, so let it go.

I told Paul that I was ready to talk about the breakup, and I guess I put on a good fake front. It had been a couple of weeks, and he still hadn't given me a reason why he dumped me like that. This time he said, "Do you really want to know?" When I said yes, he told me he had met this other girl at one of his team's away games. She went to another school, and he had been dating both of us for a few weeks. She finally made him decide—it was her or me. He picked her. Since I found out, all I can do is picture her, and wonder why he chose her over me. I wish I had never asked, and that I hadn't lied and said I was ready for his answer. It's true that ignorance is bliss.

—Ivana, 17

What to do when you just plain miss him so much you can't stand it: There are those moments when you see something on TV (his favorite actor is in a new movie, and you just have to tell him) or you remember a private joke—something that only he would get. You have to call him then—it's like a knee-jerk reaction; he's the only person who would understand. "Don't call him, whatever you do," says Rhonda Findling, psychotherapist and author of *Don't Call That Man!* "You have to break out of the habit of calling him to share new events or thoughts, so call a friend instead and tell her about your longings to call him."

If you can't resist and end up calling him anyhow, you could be making things worse for yourself. "You risk rejection," says Dr. Findling, "or worse, feeling close to him again, which could be more destructive since you're not a couple anymore. This just makes the feeling of loss even stronger when you hang up the phone." An important step to getting over him is allowing yourself to feel sad about your loss during these moments. You can't call him anymore, and that sucks, so let yourself cry if you want to. Just don't cry to him.

Other Desperate Situations

The phone isn't the only danger during this delicate post-breakup/almost-recovery time. Here are a few of the other daily problems you might be faced with and what to do about them.

What to do when you still think of him first thing every morning: During the post-breakup, some times are just plain harder than others. When you're busy concentrating on something else or hanging out with your friends, it's easier to ignore your sadness. But when you're alone, sitting in your room listening to music, it's not as easy. That's because your brain isn't occupied with any other significant thoughts, so it goes to the only thing that's really on your mind: *him*. That's why you still think of him every morning when you wake up and every night before you go to sleep. You probably find that you're thinking of him in your most boring classes, or in study hall, more than any other time of the day. That's because you have the downtime to think of him. And you need to start replacing those thoughts with other ideas and more positive images.

If you've been following the advice in this book so far, you've started some kind of new activity in the past few days or weeks. Either you just started an exercise regimen or you've been writing in a journal, or you joined a new after-school club. You need to use your new activities as a replacement for thoughts of your ex-boyfriend. Yeah, it sounds strange—How can drama club ever replace your boyfriend? Here's how: When you find yourself with downtime and your thoughts go to him, erase those images. Catch yourself and say, "I'm not going to think about him; instead I'm going to think about . . ." Then replace the thoughts of him with thoughts of whatever your new activity is. If it's running, think about the run you're going to take after school, how far you're going to go, what route you're going to take, what tape you're going to put in your Walkman, etc.

If you've started writing in a journal, take out your journal and start working on a poem or a short story. Just creating something can help take away your feelings of loss. The key to making this work is that you need to pick a "replacement" thought in advance and have it ready in the back of your mind for those weak moments. Be prepared. Tell yourself, "When I think about Eric first thing tomorrow morning, I'm going to replace thoughts of him with brainstorming ideas for my history project." It's that easy. Then when your alarm wakes you up and you find yourself thinking of him, you can instantly shut off the hurt and move on to another thought.

What to do when you're still holding out hope that you'll get back together with him: Letting go of the fantasy that you'll get back together with your ex-boyfriend isn't easy. It might be one of the hardest things you have to do in order to get over him. But allowing yourself to cling to fantasies that the two of you might get back together is only going to hurt you and set back your heartbreak recovery. Here's why:

It's painful: Thinking about him all the time, even if it's just wondering about the chances of a reunion, will be hurtful for you. *It's a waste of your energy:* You're supposed to be devoting your time to working on yourself, making yourself a better person. If you're sitting around daydreaming about getting back together with him, you're just wasting time that could be spent on a million other, more useful things. Haven't you wasted enough time on him already?

It puts you in reverse: You need to be moving forward, not backward. Every time you imagine yourself getting back together with him, you're setting yourself back days or weeks when it comes to your recovery time. Your fantasies will keep you from saying to yourself and to the outside world that it's over—an idea you have got to get used to in order to feel better.

One more little hint on this topic: Every time you start imagining that the two of you might get back together, just remember he knows your number, he sees you at school, he dumped YOU. If he wanted you back, why wouldn't he just tell you? And why would you want to get back together with someone who could so easily hurt you? You know the answer to that.

Chapter Eight

Almost over Him —But No One Cares

So your big breakup is no longer the hot gossip at school. It's been a few weeks, and everyone but you has sort of forgotten about it. Maybe even your best friend—the one who's been there for you through everything—has started saying: "Why don't you just forget that guy?" Easy for her to say!

When your ex-boyfriend and all your friends are ready to move on after the breakup and you're still hurting, you have a couple of options. One choice is to put on a brave face and pretend you're totally over him. When his name comes up in conversation, you can say, "Doug who?" as if you have no idea who the guy is anymore. But that option is false, and it does nothing to actually help you get over your ex. The other option is to look deep inside yourself and try to figure out why this is taking so long. Shouldn't you feel better by now? Maybe; maybe not. It takes a while to really get back to your old self after a breakup, and sometimes you might feel stuck—or as though you're never going to fully recover. The truth is that you *will* feel completely over him one day. Right now, let's find out what's holding you back so that you can fix it and keep moving ahead.

Look Deep: Since this pain is emotional, it's all contained inside of you—your heart and your mind hold the secrets to your sadness, and the keys to your recovery. So, even if you feel as if your emotions are a mystery to you, they're not. You actually do know the answer to why it's taking so long to move on; you just need the courage to look inside yourself and grab it. Think hard, and be very honest with yourself.

Remember, it's just you and yourself—no one else has to know what you're thinking.

It might be helpful to meditate or spend an hour alone, cutting out all outside distractions. Just sit quietly and let the thoughts of your ex-boyfriend and that relationship come into your mind. What do you see? Are you hung up on him because he was the first guy you had sex with—and now you're regretting that choice? Or is it that he left you for someone else, and you're feeling inadequate somehow? Whatever the reason, you can't truly get over him and your breakup until you face the truth about how you feel. You, and you alone, know the answer to the question: Why is it taking me so long to get over this?

Hiding at Home: One of the last steps to recovery is getting out there again. Are you camping out in your room on Saturday nights? Sure, it would be terrible to run into him at the movies with his new girlfriend, but if it's going to happen you might as well be ready to face it. You can't hide from him forever.

If you find that you're not invited to certain parties because a friend invited him instead of you, the worst thing to do is sit at home moping about it. Don't punish yourself when you did nothing wrong. Invent your own good time—go with your best friend to the mall and get a makeover at the makeup counter or check out a movie instead.

If you're scared to go to a party or a school event—like a football game—because you think he might be there, it's time to get brave. The first couple of weeks after a breakup, it's okay to isolate yourself. It might not be healthy for you to see him then. But once you're feeling ready to move on, it's time to reclaim some of those "couple" activities and places as your own again. Don't be afraid to walk down a certain hallway at school because his locker is there. And don't arrange your weekend activities around avoiding him. Truly being over him means that you don't consider him or what he's doing this weekend when you make your plans. You're too busy making plans for you.

Your Fantasy: Since no one but you knows what you're really thinking, this step requires total honesty. Are you still secretly fantasizing that you and he will get back together? Of course you are. Surprised that we knew that? Don't be. Everyone goes through it. Even if it's a deep, dark secret that you wouldn't tell your best friend, you're still imagining that somehow, against all odds, you two will be reunited—even if it takes years. Maybe you'll be away at college, and when you come home he'll want to see you . . . and the fantasy spins out from there.

It's totally normal to imagine this—and to wish for it. A reunion makes perfect sense in your mind and your heart. He went away, and you started hurting. If he comes back, the hurting will stop, right? But in reality, you know it's not that simple. Think realistically:

What if your fantasy came true and you two were reunited? What then? Would you ever be able to trust him again—or would you be constantly worried that he was going to hurt you as he did before? And would you ever regain the innocent love you enjoyed the first time around? The problems that broke you up the first time would probably still be there to destroy your relationship a second time. If you two were ever meant to be back together, it would be in a totally new relationship as two totally different people.

When your reunion fantasies start creeping in, remember that what you have been through as a part of this breakup has changed you forever. If the two of you are meant to be together again, it won't be a fantasy and it won't be just the way it used to be. Accept that, and drop the fantasy—once and for all.

Sad about the End of Sadness

When you're nearing the point of almost

being over him totally, the end of your mourning can trigger a whole new set of feelings. As crazy as it sounds, it's as though you're sad about the end of being sad. Here's how one girl put these feelings into words:

Slowly, I just stopped thinking about him. I was able to wake up in the morning and think about something else: the test I had in English that day, or what I was doing that night. I realized it all at once, that he wasn't the only thing I thought about anymore. But instead of being happy about it, that just made me sad. It really was totally over. He wasn't coming back. We had both just moved on. It was like I was finally facing the death of our love.

—Lucy, 16

It isn't easy to face your new single life with a huge smile on your face. But here are five things to remind you that moving on to the next level is something to celebrate. Don't be afraid to embrace the new you and leave your sadness behind.

Your Best Bud Rocks

Think about all the friends you've been hanging out with whom you never had time for when you were his girlfriend. And realize that your awesome best friend has been through this whole mess with you—from taking a backseat when you had a boyfriend all the way through listening to you cry in the middle of night. You've tested your friendship with her and all your other friends and family. You are so lucky to have these people in your life—you know now that you can always count on them, no matter what.

You Know Yourself and Can Be Yourself

Admit it: even though you might have thought it was a little silly to start writing poetry or jotting down your feelings in a journal every day, you're way more in touch with yourself now than you ever were before. You know that if you want to have a good cry, you can and that it will make you feel better. You know how to get in touch with your true feelings and work on getting over them. You know that if you have your heart broken, you will go on living. Best of all, you believe now that you can and will get over this guy—and that you'll fall in love again with someone new in the future.

Change Your Look

Remember how you wanted to go chop your hair off the day he broke up with you? Well, now you're stable enough to get that makeover—if you still want it. If you feel like shedding the "old" you, go ahead. Get a haircut, or try some temporary hair color. Change your lip gloss to a new funky, glittery shade for a day. Try out new looks and remember that the clothes you wear and what you do with your hair are your choice; it's not about him anymore. Who cares what he thinks?

Read Your Journal

Look back to the first page in your breakup journal and read about the feelings and emotions you were having then. Sounds like someone else, doesn't it? So, see how far you've come? That was you, just a few weeks or months ago. Now you're feeling so much better. And there's only more good stuff coming your way.

Give the New Guy a Chance

That's right: It's time to start dipping your toes in the guy pool again. Remember, you're single—you're not boyfriendless or so-and-so's ex-girlfriend; you're just single. A few weeks ago, you might have thought: "I'm never dating again." But one sure sign of recovery is when you start noticing that cute new guy in your chem class. Find out if he needs a chem lab partner and get to know him. And stop thinking about how much your ex hurt you every time you look at a new guy. Your motto when it comes to boys is: They aren't all bad!

What to do if you're still feeling sad . . .

There's a healthy limit to everything, even sadness. If you've gone through a few weeks or even months and you're really not feeling better, or if you're feeling worse and worse every day, you should talk to your parents—or to your school guidance counselor if talking with your parents seems awkward. You may need to ask for help from a professional, a doctor or therapist. This isn't anything to be ashamed of. There are millions of doctors in the world who do nothing but help people with problems like sadness and depression. That's because feeling bummed, especially when something major like a breakup has happened to you, is totally normal. And when you've got a lot of other issues going on in your life on top of your bad breakup, it's helpful to have a real specialist to talk to about your problems. Take this miniquiz and see where you are on the sadness spectrum:

1. At bedtime, you usually:

    a. Cry and think about everything that went wrong that day. It's impossible for you to fall asleep, sometimes for hours.

    b. Think about your ex-boyfriend for a little bit before you fall asleep.

    c. Fall asleep pretty quickly, within a half hour of turning out the light.

2. When it's time to get busy on your homework, you:

    a. Can focus for an hour or two, but then you need a break for a little TV.

    b. Find it hard to focus on topics that used to be your favorites. What's the point?

    c. Do some work on your favorite subject, and then call your best friend for a chat.

3. With your free time after school:

    a. What free time? You're busy with the team or the school play.

    b. You used to be on a team or the school paper, but you're just not into it anymore. Now you'd rather be left alone.

    c. You usually hang with friends, help around the house, or get an early start on homework.

4. The idea of suicide has crossed your mind:

    a. Once, when you were really bummed about something, but you realized it was a really dumb idea.

    b. Never. You wouldn't consider it—that's not a solution!

    c. Sometimes you wonder how your ex and friends would feel if they heard you had died or tried to kill yourself.

5. In the future you see yourself:

    a. Going to the college of your dreams and having a great time.

    b. It's hard for you to picture the future; you're still not sure how you're getting through tomorrow.

    c. Having a loving family of your own— with lots of kids.

6. If there were one thing you could change about your life, it would be:

    a. To have more money and be able to buy all the things you want.

    b. Your looks—you would be taller and thinner and have a perfect smile.

    c. You would be able to go back to the past, when you were happier, before all your problems started.

Scoring: Find your answers for each question and add up your points:

1. a. 3, b. 2, c. 1
2. a. 1, b. 3, c. 2
3. a. 1, b. 3, c. 2
4. a. 2, b. 1, c. 3
5. a. 1, b. 3, c. 2
6. a. 1, b. 2, c. 3

If you scored fifteen points or more on this quiz, you need to talk to your parents or someone else you trust (like a teacher or guidance counselor) right away about getting some help. You could be suffering from a serious disorder called clinical depression. According to Dr. Mark Goulston, the UCLA-based psychiatrist who has worked with MTV's *Road Rules* and *Real World* teens, "If this down feeling has gone on for more than a few weeks and has crossed over into sleeping problems (such as being unable to wake up or not being able to sleep through the night), eating problems (where you can't eat or can't stop eating), crying too easily or not at all, and not being able to concentrate or focus, you need to see your family doctor and talk about it." Your parents or family doctor can put you in touch with a therapist who can help you feel better. "And after your hurt lessens," Dr. Goulston adds, "a good therapist can help guide you on how to better handle your life and the situations that may have started you into your depression in the first place." Just having someone to talk to can be a huge help, as it was for Kim:

I felt like Joe and everyone else was moving on, like they had these busy lives and they kept going. I was standing on the side, watching them as they zoomed by and as they kept going into the distance until they disappeared. Or maybe I was the one who disappeared. I don't know. But slowly I isolated myself until I felt I had no friends, no one to talk to, and Joe was already dating someone new, a really popular girl. I started to gain weight, and for the first time in my life I just didn't care. My mom tried to talk to me, but I would just stare at her mouth moving and never listen to her. Finally, my English teacher took me aside after class. My grade had gone from about an A to a D in about three months. Ms. Maseda said to me, "I know you and Joe broke up last fall, but you need to get over him. If that's what's making you depressed, let's get you some help." It was weird to realize that there was something actually wrong with me—and that it could be cured. I couldn't see my way out of it alone. Ms. Maseda called my mom, and together they found me a therapist to talk to. I'm so glad they did!

—Kim, 17

Kim and a lot of the other girls interviewed for this book said they didn't feel comfortable talking to their parents about their love-life troubles. It's a good thing for Kim that she had a teacher who cared enough about her to step in. Even if your problems have to do with dating or romance, don't think those troubles need to be kept secret from your folks—or that they won't understand. Remember: Your parents were teenagers once, too. They've been there and may even have some good advice for you. Being sad is a normal side effect of what you've been going through, so don't feel funny or embarrassed about asking for help, especially if other people in your family have suffered from depression. There is some evidence that certain types of depression are hereditary, and as Dr. Goulston explains, "If someone else in your family has depression, that's also a sign that you may have the kind of depression that medicine will help." Talk to your parents; they might just surprise you:

My mom knew something was up, and she would always ask me what was wrong. But since I technically wasn't allowed to date yet, I knew she'd be mad if she found out that I'd secretly had a boyfriend for a whole year, and now I was depressed since he'd dumped me. I mean, how could I tell her that? I thought about suicide every day. I even got a razor and I would sit in my room and put it against my skin—on my arms or on my legs. I guess I wasn't brave enough to kill myself. I would start cutting and then I would stop when I saw blood. A friend of mine at school gave me a hot-line number for cutters, and I called. The people at the hot line were awesome and totally understood everything. It was weird—like they could read my mind. They convinced me to tell my mom what was going on— she was so sad that I had even thought about killing myself she just cried and cried. She made me understand that nothing I could ever do would be so bad that she couldn't forgive me. My mom is amazing.

—Louisa, 16

If you find that talking to your parents or even to a teacher makes you too uncomfortable, there are hot lines you can call and Web sites that offer tons of good advice. See page 133 in the back of this book and reach out to someone right away.

Chapter Nine

Can We Be Friends?

Now that you've gotten this far, there's only one emotional hurdle left. It's the task of actually trying to be friends with your ex. In high school, it's almost impossible to completely ignore someone whom you see every day. Your best bet is to at least try to be a little bit friendly. Besides, you two were once really close, so why should all those good times be erased just because you broke up?

If he was really a snake and dumped you in a horrible way, then this chapter is not for you. In fact, some ex-boyfriends are people we're better off without. If your ex falls into this category, you can work on just being civil to him—he's clearly not friendship material. But if you're in the other category, you're probably realizing that even though it didn't work out between you two, your ex is still a pretty cool guy—and someone you'd still like to hang out with. You might be looking at a future friend if you take this transition slowly and carefully and protect your heart.

Step # 1: Are You Ready?

This miniquiz will help you determine if you're ready to move into friendship mode with your ex-boyfriend.

1. When the phone rings, do you think, "It might be him!" and dive for it before anyone else can pick it up.

Y ☐   N ☐

2. Are you still secretly fantasizing that you two will get back together? (you have to be superhonest about this, otherwise you WILL get hurt again.) So, honestly, are you still daydreaming about a reunion?

Y ☐   N ☐

3. When you bump into him at school   **Y   N**
or at a party, is it still painful for you   ☐   ☐
(do you think, "I always loved him in
that blue shirt" or "How can he be
here with HER?" etc.)?

4. Does your heart pound when he seeks   **Y   N**
you out, stops by your locker, writes you   ☐   ☐
a simple e-mail? Do you feel yourself
blushing or getting nervous when
he's around?

Scoring: If you answered *yes* to any of these questions, you need more time before trying to move this broken relationship into a friendship.

Not Ready?

Sure, it's normal and okay to feel a little nervous around your ex-boyfriend, but look at it this way: Do your friends make you nervous in the same way? Didn't think so. The most important thing to remember during this phase is to be honest with yourself. If you are still fantasizing—even a little bit—that you two might get back together, you're not ready to see him. And you're the only person who knows if you're really ready. So look deep inside, and be sure before you move on to Step 2. If you have any doubt at all, it's better to wait a couple more weeks than to get hurt all over again.

Step #2: If You're Ready ...

So you answered *no* to every question on the quiz. That means you're ready, right? Be sure. If you're still not over him and you go out on a friendly date, you're going to be hurt all over again. Picture this: He's going to talk about his life, just like all your other friends, and that life may now include another girl or girlfriend. Are you ready for that? Even if he doesn't have a new girl in his life, he's going to talk about things that you used to be a part of—like his friends all hanging out, his soccer games, whatever—all stuff that you're not included in anymore. If you're ready to hear about his life going on without you, then you're ready to see him. If you don't think you are, it's best to steer clear of this for now, and try again in a few weeks.

The first step to friendship is making a date—not that kind of date! In fact, let's not even call it a date. You're simply setting up a time when you two can hang out and talk. And so that you don't send him the wrong message, it might be a good idea to do a group activity: go to the school basketball game with a group of friends, or meet at a party. If you're really ready for this step, asking him to hang out won't be awkward at all. It's not as if you were going to call him up and say, "Hi, it's me . . . your ex-girlfriend." Because if you're ready for this stage, you're already talking to him every now and then at school or around town. And you're feeling totally comfortable with him. If you haven't talked to him since you two broke up, you need to break the ice first. Say "hi" at school. Let him know you don't hate him anymore. Just be cool around him, and he'll get the idea. He probably still feels terrible about what happened—odds are he misses you and he wants to be friends, too.

The Rules

Here are some ground rules before you start hanging out with your ex.

Pick a Public Place: Do not go over to his house, or have him come over to your house. That's a big mistake. Do not pick a place that used to be yours as a couple—not your favorite restaurant or the movie theater where you had your first date. Pick a new place—or let him pick a place. But make sure you don't have any history there.

Don't Try Too Hard: If you feel a little nervous before you see him, that's normal. But if you're spending more than thirty minutes picking out just the right outfit for your meeting, then you probably aren't ready to see this guy yet.

Remember, this should feel more like you're just meeting a friend—and not like a date. So if you're trying to remember which sweater he liked best on you, or you're doing your hair the way he liked it, you need to cancel plans right away.

Play It Out: You know him; he knows you. Picture in your head what he will say when he sees you, and what you will say back. Play out a couple of imaginary conversations in your head. What kinds of questions are you comfortable asking him? (Do you want to know if he's seeing someone? Are you really ready for the answer?) This mock convo will help you feel out your own boundaries of what you're prepared to talk about during the first meeting—and what topics to stay away from.

Don't Get Physical: When you get together, you may find that you're still attracted to your old boyfriend, even though he dumped you and broke your heart. He still has those cute dimples that you love, or you had forgotten how good he looks in that blue shirt. Suddenly, the reasons behind your breakup seem blurry, and hard to remember. And he's so cute, so funny . . . *Wait.*

Whatever happens, don't let things get physical—even a hug for old times sake can turn into something you're better off without. It's hard to resist, because when you're in his presence, and he's being nice, you may be able to put all the hurt he caused you out of your mind. But if you have a make-out session with your old boyfriend on your "friendly" date, you're going to be hurt all over again. And if you have any suspicion that this guy is a user, you'll find out for sure during this reunion time. If it's clear that he only wanted to see you again because he thought he was gonna get some, your hopes of friendship are probably out of reach. Move on.

Keep It Short: Make the plans around a specific

time, and set a time limit. If you're going to see him for lunch or coffee on a Saturday, don't leave your evening plans open in case he wants to keep hanging out. You need to have plans an hour or two hours later than the time of your meeting. Make your best friend meet you right afterward, and don't be late! Keeping things on a friendship level is important—especially if after seeing him again you're feeling sad. Your best friend will be there for you, and you can tell her everything that happened. You should be the one setting the boundaries of this meeting—just being in control of the time you spend with him will make you feel more powerful.

Chapter Ten

The New Guy
& Other Good Stuff

After your first big breakup, if you're not careful, you're probably going to encounter a new kind of boyfriend. He's called the Rebound Guy. The weird thing about a rebound guy is that you're the last one to know you're dating him. Here's how it usually happens. You've just broken up with your longtime boyfriend, and you're feeling pretty low. A guy whom you never gave much thought to suddenly asks you to the Homecoming Dance. Everyone tells you that you should go, it would be good for you. So you do. OR: There's a guy who's like your best friend—you can tell him anything. And after your bad breakup, this guy friend becomes your constant companion. Before you know it, he's calling you his girlfriend. You don't have an amazing time with this guy—he's not like your old boyfriend. But he's a great friend, and it's safer to be dating a friend than someone you're really in love with, right? He tells you that you're pretty. And it is nice to have a date—to have someone want to take you out and boost your confidence.

So what's wrong with a rebound guy? The problem is that he might have real feelings for you, while you're probably just using him as a distraction (whether you're doing it on purpose or not). A safe way to avoid hurting anyone's feelings is to be sure you're really ready to start dating again before you go out with anyone. If you're at the point where you can see your ex-boyfriend as a friend, you're probably ready to date new people. But take the little test on the following page just to be sure:

Why do you want a boyfriend?

(Finish this sentence by picking two answers that sound the most like you.)

I want a boyfriend . . .

so I have someone to hang out with..............2 points

to go to the school dance with ....5 points

so other people won't think I'm a loser ....5 points

because I'm lonely ....2 points

because I want someone to have fun with ......2 points

to make my ex-boyfriend jealous ....10 points

because all my friends have boyfriends..........5 points

to escape from my parents........................10 points

Scoring: Look at the points after the two answers you picked. Add the numbers together for your total.

If you scored anywhere below ten points, you're probably ready to start dating again. Your motives for wanting a guy in your life are solid, honest, and—best of all—totally normal.

If you scored ten or above, you might need a little bit more time. A "little bit more time" doesn't mean that you have to lock yourself away in your room; it just means that you should give yourself a few weeks. Try it and see—in a couple of weeks you probably won't be feeling so vulnerable. You'll have the wisdom to turn down a date with any potential rebound guy because you'll realize that your motives for dating him are wrong and possibly hurtful. You'll probably also find that any guy whom you were crushing on a few weeks ago might start looking a little less appealing. That's a good sign, too—it means you won't settle for anything less than what you deserve. And right now, you deserve a lot—especially for getting over guy #1.

The Good News

There is a good—or even great—side to every breakup. It's hard to see the sunshine ahead while in you're in the clouds of your sadness, but it is coming. Here's what you have to look forward to:

You are stronger now. The old saying is true: That which doesn't kill you makes you stronger. You've come close to having your heart and soul ripped out, and yet you were a strong enough person to survive. Did you ever think you could live through something like this? You've been tested now, and you know that you can handle just about anything.

You know what you want. Being dumped has forced you to reevaluate what you want in a boyfriend—and what you simply won't settle for. You've analyzed your last relationship in great detail, and that's a good thing. You know now what you can handle, and what isn't for you. You're also better able to find a more satisfying relationship with your next boyfriend.

You know you're also okay on your own. And what about being single? It's not so bad! You know now that the world isn't going to end if you don't have a date for the prom. You must be able to count on yourself, because sometimes other people—even your best friends—will let you down. Be strong and stay single until someone who is really worthy of you comes along.

Nothing hurts like the first time. You'll hear this from a lot of older people—like your mom or your older sister. There is no heartbreak like the first heartbreak. It's just like the first time you do anything—it's scary, and you don't know how it's going to turn out. But next time your love life turns sour, you'll be able to look back on these days and say, "I got through it then and even fell in love again." Just knowing you've lived through a heartbreak once is enough to keep you going.

More Good News

The girls interviewed for this book were asked one question at the end of the interview: Is there anything good that came out of your breakup? It sounds ridiculous—what could be good about being dumped and having your heart broken? Well, actually, a lot of things. Here's what the girls said, in their own words.

The first thing I did when Kev broke up with me was to call my best friend, Shelia. She said she felt sorry for me, but then she went on to say that Kev was really a huge loser and she had never liked him anyhow. That hurt. Even though I was mad at Kev right then, I needed her to console me, not bad-mouth him. As it turns out, I ended up not hanging out with Shelia but spending a lot of time with this girl I didn't even consider a close friend of mine. She was in my art class, and she just came up to me one day and said she had been dumped last year and how hard it was for her. She offered to talk anytime I needed to. We started eating lunch together, and a lot of the time I would just start crying because Kev had the same lunch period as me and I would see him sitting with his new girlfriend. While Shelia was like "Just forget about him," my new friend, Katie, really understood. Anyhow, in the end I made a great new friend. That was two years ago, and

Katie and I are still best buds. I couldn't have done it without her.

—Suzanne, 18

After Jeremy, I thought I would never fall in love again. I trusted him so much, and then he hurt me, so I didn't want to get that close to anyone ever again. When school started senior year, I had already decided I was just going to do my homework, study, and do the school drama club and that's it for senior year—no boyfriends. But there was this new guy at school named Max, who ended up in drama club, too. He was only a junior, but everybody was crazy about him. He was supercute, but as I said, I just wasn't interested. After two months of rehearsing this one play, we got to be friends and I learned a lot about him. Finally one night he asked me out. My impulse was to say yes. I really was getting into him, but then I'd think about what happened with Jeremy. So I just said no. I told Max about Jeremy, and he understood. He even said he would wait for me until I was ready to date again. And he did wait. He didn't date anyone all year , and we just got closer and closer. At the end of the year, we were like best friends, and I knew I could trust him with my heart. I asked him to prom and had the most amazing night. Max has taught me that not everyone is like Jeremy—demanding and cruel—and that I can have a real love in my life without it turning everything else rotten. I'm really in love, thanks to Max.

—Lane, 19

I took my friend's advice after my bad breakup with Tommy, and I started writing poems about it. Every day when I had a spare minute or two, I would work on a poem. Some of the poems were angry, and some were sad. I think I spent months just filling notebook after notebook with poems. When we did a poetry unit in English class, I was so into it. I started borrowing poetry books from the teacher, and I showed her my notebooks of poems. She read a couple of the better ones and told me I had real talent! To make a long story short, I just had a poem of mine published in the *school literary journal, and everyone at school has complimented me on it. I think I found my true calling—and all because that jerk decided to lie to me and dump me. All I have to say is: That's great!*

—Beth, 16

Paul broke up with me over the phone, after sending me a mean e-mail. First, I was just in shock. I had dated him for almost two years. And now he just wanted to dump me for someone else. Well, it's taken me a long time to get over him and a long, long time to ever trust anyone again. But now I have a great new guy in my life who I totally trust with my heart. What I learned from Paul is that I would never, ever hurt anyone the way he hurt me. And I'm much more considerate. I know just how it feels to be dumped. If I needed to break up with a guy, I would be so caring about it—and gentle. Paul taught me how cruel people can be, and I don't ever want to be like him.

—Louisa, 16

The End

So here you are, at the end of this book and probably at the end of your broken heart. Look at how far you've come and all the things you've learned about yourself—and about love. Congratulations! It's time for you to use everything you've learned from this experience to help yourself and others. When you fall in love again (and yes, you will fall in love again!) remember how lucky you are to have the confidence in yourself that allows you to share love and trust with another person. And when your best friend or your little sister gets her heart broken, be there for her, just as you wanted someone with you during your breakup. Teach her the most important thing you've learned from your own hard times: The greatest love in the world is the love you have for yourself.

P.S.

If you want to read more about how to handle bad breakups and other probs, turn the page to find some cool books and great resources.

Resources

Help Line Directory

If you feel that you need someone to talk to, you're not alone. There are a lot of help lines and Web sites where you can find great advice to get through the bad times. To start with, try one of these help lines. Don't wait until it's too late; reach out and get help now:

For depression and extreme sadness: 800-826-3632 (National Depression Association)

If you're injuring yourself: 800-DONT-CUT (SAFE, Self Abuse Finally Ends)

For suicidal thoughts: 800-HIT-HOME (Youth Crisis Hotline)

If you have questions about sexual relationships: 888-396-LINE (Teen Reproductive Health Hotline)

Books

If you want to read more about relationships (or even Karma!), here are some of the titles mentioned in this book that you might want to look for:

Don't Call That Man! A Survival Guide to Letting Go, by Rhonda Fieldling, Hyperion, 1999.

Get Out of Your Own Way: Overcoming Self-Defeating Behavior, by Mark Goulston, M.D., and Philip Goldberg, Perigee, 1996.

Karma Manual: Nine Days to Change Your Life, by Dr. Jonn Mumford and Meghan Stevens, Llewellyn World Wide, 1999.

Teen Angst? Naaah: A Quasi-Autobiography, by Ned Vizzini, Free Spirit Publishing, 2000.

Good Reads

Think you're the only one with a broken heart? Think again. These novels were all recommended by the girls we interviewed for this book. If you're looking for a good read about love and loss, try one of these.

Fifteen, by Beverly Cleary, Morrow/Avon/Camelot, 1956.
"Deals with love and laughter; a funny book."—Maggie, 15

Forever, by Judy Blume, Simon & Schuster/Pocket, 1982.
*"This is the story of one girl's first true love and how she deals
with it."*—Lane, 19

Healing Hearts: Compassionate Writers on Breaking Up, edited by
John Miller and Aaron Kenedi, Morrow, 2000.
"Good short stories about breakups."—Carol, 17

Missing Angel Juan, by Francesca Lia Block,
HarperCollins, 1995.
"An amazing love story about love and loss and longing."—Kim, 17

My Darling, My Hamburger, by Paul Zindel, Bantam Starfire,
1984.
*"Follows two couples: one couple gets the whole love thing right, the
other couple screws everything up. A really good book."*—Maggie, 15

Rilke on Love and Other Difficulties, by Rainer Maria Rilke,
W.W. Norton, 1994.
"Amazing poems about life and love; really beautiful."—Kim, 17

Stargirl, by Jerry Spinelli, Knopf, 2000.
*"Told from the guy's perspective, he tries to change his girlfriend and
ends up losing her. He never gets over it."*—Len, 17

CYLIN BUSBY

has officially been dumped twice,
once in high school (reason: he cheated)
and once in college (he wanted to "still be friends").
Now the Senior Editor at Teen Magazine,
Cylin is also the author of several young adult novels
and numerous articles. She lives in Los Angeles
with her husband, Damon.